CREDITS AND COLLECTIONS

Techniques to Improve Your Cash Flow

Candace Mondello

A FIFTY-MINUTE™ SERIES BOOK

CRISP PUBLICATIONS, INC.
Menlo Park, California

CREDITS AND COLLECTIONS
Techniques To Improve Your Cash Flow

Candace Mondello

CREDITS
Editor: **Elaine Brett**
Layout and Composition: **Interface Studio**
Cover Design: **Carol Harris**
Artwork: **Ralph Mapson**

Copyright © 1991 by Crisp Publications, Inc.
Printed in the United States of America

English language Crisp books are distributed worldwide. Our major international distributors include:

CANADA: Reid Publishing, Ltd., Box 69559—109 Thomas St., Oakville, Ontario Canada L6J 7R4. TEL: (416) 842-4428; FAX: (416) 842-9327

AUSTRALIA: Career Builders, P.O. Box 1051, Springwood, Brisbane, Queensland, Australia 4127. TEL: 841-1061, FAX: 841-1580

NEW ZEALAND: Career Builders, P.O. Box 571, Manurewa, Auckland, New Zealand. TEL: 266-5276, FAX: 266-4152

JAPAN: Phoenix Associates Co., Mizuho Bldg. 2-12-2, Kami Osaki, Shinagawa-Ku, Tokyo 141, Japan. TEL: 3-443-7231, FAX: 3-443-7640

Selected Crisp titles are also available in other languages. Contact International Rights Manager Suzanne Kelly at (415) 323-6100 for more information.

This book is printed on recyclable paper with soy ink.

Library of Congress Catalog Card Number 90-84234
Mondello, Candace
Credits and Collections
ISBN 1-56052-080-9

PREFACE

Okay, empty your pockets. How much cash do you have on you?* Enough for a meal? Enough for a full tank of gas? Enough for this week's groceries or—more to the point—this month's accounts payable?

Credit is part of everybody's everyday life. Since you can't escape it, you have to learn to manage it. This book will show you how to do just that.

You'll learn:

- Why credit and collections are becoming increasingly important

- How to develop a profitable credit strategy

- How to identify profitable credit customers

- How to avoid most major credit problems

- How to deal with major collection problems

Remember, money doesn't make the world go around. *Credit* makes the world go around. You can use the techniques in this book to keep your own little world turning smoothly.

Candace L. Mondello

Candace Mondello

---

*No, checks *don't* count. As anyone who's ever taken a bad check will tell you, cash and checks are not the same thing.

CONTENTS

(Contents continued overleaf)

C H A P T E R

1

Why Is Credit
So Important?

Credit is a spider web, a fragile thread that is bound to (and affected by) virtually all business components—the outside business environment, your competitors, your customers, and your own internal systems and philosophies.

If you understand what credit is all about and why it's so important, chances are you can set up profitable spinoffs.

THE CREDIT ENVIRONMENT

There are lots of players in the credit field and they affect the way businesses like yours play the game. Some that are outside your control or influence can make it tough to play with the Big Boys. Let's take a look at some facts about how two major players affect your company's credit situation.

PLAYER #1: The General Business Environment

- Bank credit is getting harder to come by.

  Problems within the banking industry (a slowing economy, stronger government regulations, bad or underperforming portfolios, etc.) are forcing banks to limit credit to current customers. Old loans are being called in and new loans are being denied. Banks can't lend out what they don't have.

  When customers can't get bank credit they turn to *their* "lender of last resort." No, not the Federal Reserve System—*your accounts receivables department.*

- Local conditions exacerbate credit problems.

  Let's say a major local employer—a manufacturer—goes under. You run a popular stationery store. You'll lose the company's business. You'll lose retail customers as its former employees move away. You'll lose business as the small service and retail shops supported by the manufacturer and its employees close down. Your business spirals down in a vicious circle.

Ironically, both local recessions and local expansions can strain your credit system to its breaking point. Since you don't control the economy, you have to go with the cash flow.

PLAYER #2: Specific Business Environment

- Competitors can create a credit nightmare.

  Sample scenario: You sell a top-quality product at a fair price. Unfortunately, customers see your widget as a commodity—one they could easily buy from your competitors. Product differentiation appears impossible.

  Your competitors decide to compete via credit differentiation. They know that price isn't everything. Credit and payment terms can be much more influential in the buying decision. Examples:

  - Competitor A offers payment terms of 2/10 net 30. That discount rate translates to an equivalent percent/year of 36%. If a buyer can get financing at less than 36% interest, he's money ahead to borrow from somebody else* and pay A immediately.

  - Competitor B offers payment terms of net 60. Interest at 18% per annum is charged on all accounts over 61 days old. In short, the customer gets a free 60-day loan.

  - Competitor C offers a C.O.D. discount deal of 5%. That's a tremendous price break on a "commodity."

  Competitor credit campaigns influence the kind and amount of credit you extend to customers. You'll need a good credit pitch if you want to stay in their league.

So what does this typical scenario mean? Credit decisions aren't something you make in a vacuum. They're something you make in potentially hostile territory!

---

*He may "borrow" that money from sums set aside to pay his other bills.

THE CUSTOMER COMPONENT

There's no getting around it. Customers like credit. Even if they don't want to use it, they want to feel like it's there for the taking (and the taking advantage of!).

Credit means a lot of things to customers. Among the most important reasons for using credit are:

1. *For convenience.* Paying bills in cash is a pain. It's easier to pay one bill a month than it is to pay cash every time you need something. Carrying cash can be dangerous as well as inconvenient.

2. *No cash is available.* It's a simple premise: I don't have the money now but I want the product now. Given a choice, most customers would rather ''pay'' with credit than postpone purchases.

3. *No other credit is available.* Translation: Nobody will lend me the money to buy your product so—if you want a sale—*you* have to lend it to me.

4. *To hold creditors captive.* Many customers buy on credit because it gives them a hold on their vendors (''I'm not paying my bill until you...''). They believe credit leads to more vendor commitment, better service, faster problem resolution, and so on.

5. *For expansion.* Growing businesses often have cash-flow problems. Your credit can help them bridge their A/R-to-cash gap.

6. *For accounts payable management.* If you can pay $1000 now or pay $1000 in 45 days, you might as well take your time. There's no profit in promptness.

7. *Verification/paper trail.* Cash purchases are notoriously hard to document. A/P records, however, document every important who (who ordered the product), what (what was purchased), when (purchase date), where (delivery site), why (why the bill totaled ''X'' dollars), and how (how the bill was paid—as a lump sum, in installments, sans discount or finance charges).

8. *Ego.* Offering credit, more than anything else, is a vendor's way of demonstrating faith in a customer. Money talks, but credit **yells!**

Obviously, customers consider credit a serious business. Smart vendors do too. After all, we're all in this together.

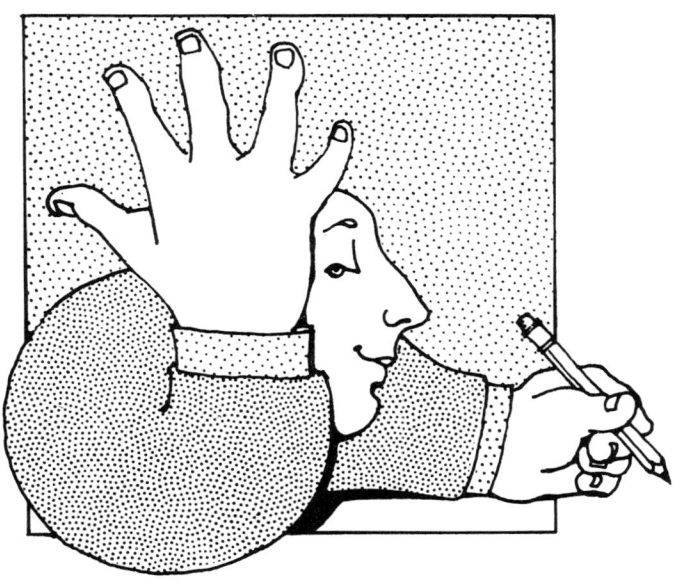

HOW MANY REASONS CAN YOU LIST WHY CUSTOMERS LIKE CREDIT?

GIVE YOURSELF CREDIT

As we've seen, customers want credit. There are many reasons you want to give it to them:

- **To provide customer service.** We've seen that customers want credit. Isn't "giving customers what they want" what business is all about?

- **To gain sales.** Many companies can't pay cash. Period. But they *can and will pay*. Do you want to lose their business?

- **To increase profits at the margin.** Economists call this concept "economies of scale." Generally, the more units you produce or sell, the lower your per-unit cost. Ergo, when credit increases your aggregate business, it also increases the profit-per-unit. Credit, in this respect, almost pays for itself.

- **To reach a broader spectrum of customers.** Cash-only payment policies often freeze out both ends of the business spectrum. Large bureaucratic businesses won't pay cash. Small, cash-poor companies can't pay cash. Credit allows you to expand your customer base.

- **To get higher prices.** Customers expect to pay for credit. They pay in the form of lost discounts, interest charges, higher product prices (cash-only companies are often discounters), minimum order lots, and so on. Their loss (cost) is your gain (income).

- **To obtain customer loyalty.** Credit demonstrates your loyalty to customers. They'll usually respond in kind.

- **To compete.** As we saw earlier in this chapter, a strong credit program is a good marketing tool. It's easier to analyze and evaluate than intangibles such as product value or quality or customer service.

- **To have a positive company image.** The issue may not be "Can I afford to offer credit?" The question may be "Can I afford *not* to?" You can't afford to have your business look less successful or less receptive to customer needs than your competitors'.

Credit is more than just a service. It's a mirror of your business. It had better give a flattering picture.

SUMMARY: WHY CREDIT IS IMPORTANT

There is no denying that credit holds an important place in business.

In the first place, it acknowledges the reality of the marketplace. Financial institutions can't or won't always provide the credit that customers need. That credit has to come from somebody. You.

In the second place, credit acknowledges the importance of giving customers what they want or need. In this case, they want and need credit so that they can buy your products.

In the third place, credit improves your business. You can benefit from greater sales, higher aggregate and per-unit profits, a broader customer base, and so on. This wide range of benefits is not available from any other business function.

Clearly, credit programs should have a place in your business—first place, because they can create big profits on your P&L.

"WE BELIEVE IN CREDIT"

C H A P T E R

2

Developing
A Super System

The first step in developing a good—or better—credit and collections (C&C) system is defining what you think a good system is.

There is no perfect C&C system. There is simply the best system for *your* business. To find that best system, start with the system you have now—the system you thought was good enough to implement! The form presented in this chapter will help you put your current system on paper.

DEVELOPING A SUPER SYSTEM

Study the Credit and Collection Policies Compilation Form (hereafter referred to as The Form) beginning on the facing page and complete it as best you can.* Add extra sheets of paper if necessary. Write N/A—Not Applicable—for issues you either have not considered or have dismissed.

Complete the form in pencil. This completed form is not your final draft. It's just a starting point.

The second step in developing your good—or better!—credit and collections system will be to address and analyze important points on The Form. Subsequent chapters provide information that will help you identify:

- Components of your current system that should remain in your finalized credit program

- Components that should play a greater or smaller role in your C&C picture

The third and final step in building a superior system will be to amend your original Form to reflect the ideas and input you've acquired. You'll be glad you did the first draft in pencil!

8 pages from now you'll have something that 90 percent of other businesses don't: a written credit policy. At this point it's just an initial draft, but it's better—*much, much better*—than nothing.

By the time you've finished this book and amended The Form, you'll have the single most crucial component of successful C&C work: a written, realistic (rather than idealistic) approach to the subject.

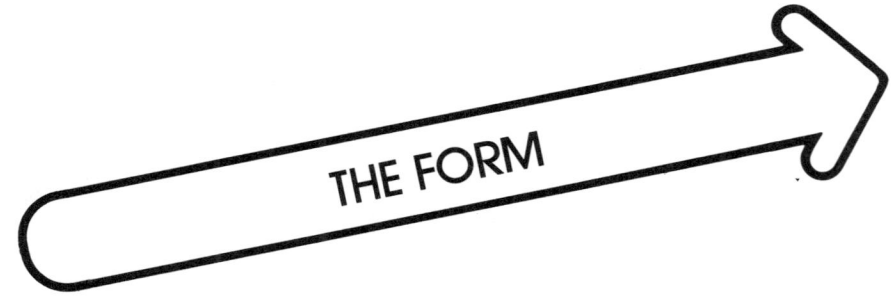

---

*If you have a high tolerance for mortification, have someone in your C&C department do the same. Chances are, the two of you see (and probably practice) the system in totally different ways. You may find that your current system isn't working because it isn't being used.

CREDIT AND COLLECTION POLICIES
THE FORM

GENERAL ADMINISTRATIVE ISSUES

• The following people are responsible for setting up the company's C&C program:

_____

_____

• Regular reviews of the policy will be made every: _____

• A supplemental review will be made under the following conditions:

_____

_____

• The criteria for measuring the effectiveness of the C&C program are:

_____

_____

_____

_____

_____

• Communicating the C&C program is the responsibility of:

_____

_____

_____

THE FORM (Continued)

CULTURAL CONCERNS

- How restrictive (e.g., liberal or conservative or somewhere in between) is our credit policy? Provide examples:

  _____
  _____
  _____

- Is our C&C program active or passive? Provide examples:

  _____
  _____
  _____

- We are comfortable with a debt level of:

  _____
  _____

- Our absolute debt level will change in accordance with the following conditions:

  _____
  _____
  _____

- We would describe our aversion to risk as being:

  _____
  _____

  Examples of risks and our response:

  _____

- We would describe the amount of structure in our C&C system as:

  _____

  Examples of structure/need for structure:

  _____
  _____

THE CREDIT PROGRAM

- Describe the billing process in depth:

  _____

  _____

  _____

  _____

- Our payment terms are: _____

- We offer these exact discount terms because: _____

  _____

  _____

- We offer net _____ days because: _____

  _____

  _____

- We charge interest on past-due accounts in the amount of:

  _____

- Interest begins accruing under what conditions: _____

  _____

  _____

  _____

  _____

- We charge this level of interest because: _____

  _____

- We impose a minimum interest charge in the amount of: _____

  _____

- We add this specific minimum charge because: _____

  _____

THE FORM (Continued)

ACCEPTABLE CLIENT DOCUMENTATION

- To be acceptable, applications must:

_____

_____

_____

- To be acceptable, applicants must furnish the following financial information:

_____

_____

_____

- To be acceptable, the following conditions must be met in regard to credit references:

_____

_____

_____

- To be acceptable, we need documentation of the following from reputable credit reporting companies:

_____

_____

_____

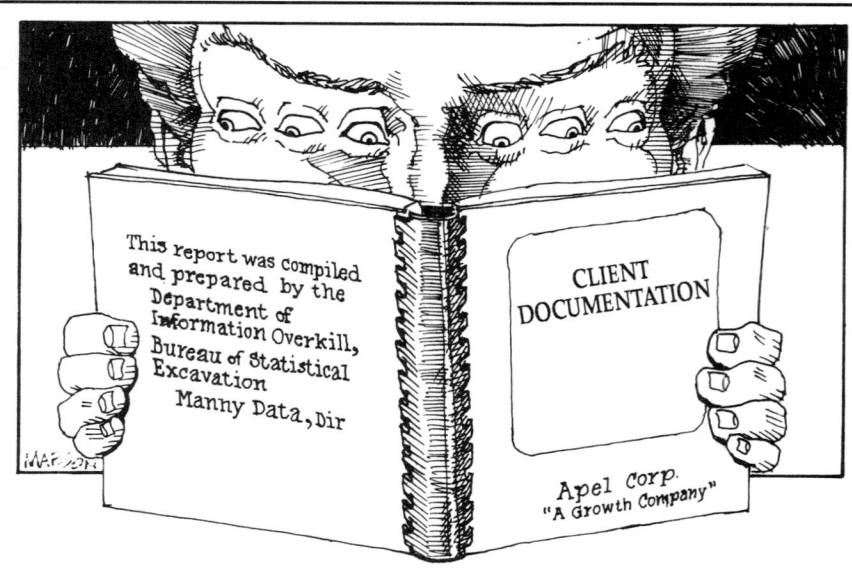

This report was compiled and prepared by the Department of Information Overkill, Bureau of Statistical Excavation

Manny Data, Dir

CLIENT DOCUMENTATION

Apel Corp. "A Growth Company"

THE FORM (Continued)

RISK CONTROL

- We ask potential customers to provide personal guarantees under the following conditions:

  _____

  _____

  _____

  _____

- We ask potential customers to provide irrevocable LCs (letters of credit) under the following conditions:

  _____

  _____

  _____

  _____

- We ask potential customers to pledge collateral under the following conditions:

  _____

  _____

  _____

  _____

- We ask potential customers to find cosigners for their accounts under the following conditions:

  _____

  _____

  _____

  _____

- Credit insurance is part of our risk abatement program (yes or no):

  _____

  _____

  _____

  _____

THE FORM (Continued)

COLLECTION SYSTEMS

- We use the following system to identify past-due accounts:

  _____

  _____

- We take first action on a past-due account when the account:

  _____

  _____

  _____

- First contact will be a:

  _____

  _____

- We will tell the customer:

  _____

  _____

- If the customer is nonresponsive, we:

  _____

  _____

- We contact the client a second time when the account:

  _____

  _____

- Second contact will be a:

  _____

- We will tell the customer:

  _____

  _____

- If the customer is nonresponsive, we:

  _____

  _____

- We contact the client a third time when the account:

  _____

  _____

- Third contact will be a:

  _____

  _____

- We will tell the customer:

  _____

  _____

  _____

- If the customer is nonresponsive, we:

  _____

  _____

  _____

- If clients try to make unauthorized partial payments, we:

  _____

  _____

  _____

- If customers refuse to pay or delay payment because they have product quality complaints, we:

  _____

  _____

  _____

- If customers refuse to pay or delay payment because of a warranty disagreement, we:

  _____

  _____

  _____

THE FORM (Continued)

COLLECTION SYSTEMS (Continued)

- If customers refuse to pay or delay payment because of an error on shipping dates, we: _____
_____
_____

- If customers refuse to pay or delay payment because of errors in the shipment (wrong product, wrong quantity, etc.), we: _____
_____
_____

- If customers refuse to pay or delay payment because they claim to be returning the product, we: _____
_____
_____

- If a customer is clearly just stalling for time (for example, he or she presents one excuse after another), we: _____
_____
_____

- We will turn an account over to a collection agency under the following conditions: _____
_____
_____

- We will turn an account over to an attorney under the following conditions:
_____
_____
_____

- We will write off an account under the following conditions:
_____
_____
_____

A WARNING: AS YOU BEGIN DEVELOPING A SUPER SYSTEM

The draft C&C program you've just outlined gives you a solid point of beginning. Chapters 3 through 8 of this book will give you pointers on how to improve each component of your plan.

But to say it point blank, the effort you put into completing this form is what will separate the men from the boys (and the women from the girls). Kids-at-heart will ignore the form and childishly go in search of The Perfect Collection Letter or The Credit Technique To End All Credit Techniques.

Those with a grown-up view all acknowledge that business knows no quick fix—not in credit and collections, not in employee relations, *not in any department*. They recognize that a sound foundation and structure is critical to any department's success.

If you don't think you gave The Form sufficient thought, please give it a second shot. It's better than shooting yourself in the foot.

"DON'T CLOWN WITH 'THE FORM'!"

C H A P T E R

3

General Administrative Issues

CREDIT DEPARTMENT PLEASE

There are basic building-block issues that need to be addressed before you fine tune the nuts-and-bolts of your C&C system. Give them their due. They are what separate the long-term success from the systematic mess.

ISSUE #1: RESPONSIBILITY FOR SETTING UP THE COMPANY'S C&C PROGRAM

Business is a team sport. Sure, there are some players in the trenches who seem more important than others (for example, there is the chief executive officer—the leader—who calls the major plays). But it's important to remember that without the team *they are nothing.* Except unemployed.

Developing a credit and collections policy should be a team effort. C&C strategies affect virtually every other business function. For example:

- *Advertising.* Companies with liberal credit policies generally do far more advertising than companies with conservative cultures.

- *Sales.* Credit restrictions often limit the amount of product a rep can sell to his or her clients.

- *Finance.* Finance departments live and breathe cash flow (that is, how much money is coming in versus going out). To those in the financial field, collections (incoming money) are a daily concern.

- *Planning.* Will we be able to bill and collect enough money to expand? Buy new equipment? Introduce new product lines? How would C&C affect...

Yes, you want a C&C specialist or top manager in charge of *finalizing* the policy (you want a quarterback, not a waterboy, calling the plays). But all parties influenced by the C&C system should have some *input* into its design. This ensures that:

- All concerns are addressed.

- The policy has universal support. (Are you more likely to support a policy you helped develop or one that was crammed down your throat?)

BOTTOM LINE: Allow all affected departments to have their C&C say. And give their say a careful listening.

ISSUE #2: REGULAR POLICY REVIEWS

Ironically, many businesspeople who insist on monthly financial statements, weekly sales reports, quarterly progress reviews, and so on, think that setting up a C&C policy is a one-shot deal.

It isn't. You should review your C&C policy regularly. *Regularly* could be defined as:

- Quarterly

- Semiannually

- Annually

- Biannually

    OR...

- Whenever there are substantial changes in:
    - ► Local unemployment figures (particularly if you run a retail business)
    - ► Economic conditions (recession, depression, expansion, local growth/contraction in customer base, etc.)
    - ► Competitors' C&C policies
    - ► Competitors' non-C&C package (can your C&C policy help reduce a competitor's gain from new products, lower prices, better warranties, etc.)
    - ► Profitability
    - ► Cash flow
    - ► Total bad debt
    - ► Average age of outstanding debts
    - ► Sales figures (is the credit policy too restrictive, choking off sales?)
    - ► Number of internal complaints about your C&C
    - ► Number of external complaints about your C&C
    - ► C&C department turnover

    NOTE: Specific conditions can be positive or negative, causing you to ease or restrict credit availability.

> **BOTTOM LINE:** C&C policies must change with the times. Determine when and/or under what conditions you will review C&C policies. *Then do it.*

ISSUE #3: MEASURING THE EFFECTIVENESS OF THE C&C PROGRAM

It's easy to measure the effectiveness of a C&C program, right? Rapid cash flow and no bad debts. Simplicity itself!

Unfortunately, in this case the KISS (Keep It Simple, Stupid) method kisses off potential profits. If a company is to succeed, it must go beyond sure things. Writing off a few bad debts is a part of doing business.

Evaluate your C&C system as a whole. There are many measures of C&C effectiveness, including:

- Bad debt as a percentage of sales

- Bad debt as a percentage of A/R

- Losses in absolute dollars

- Number of bad accounts

- Number of account writedowns (how many accounts did you have to negotiate down to get any payment at all?)

- Account writedowns in absolute dollars

- Account writedowns as a percentage of A/R

- Average age of A/R

The above measurements can be combined for more detailed analyses. Use these measurements to compare your record to industry averages, competitors' figures, other local companies' figures, etc.

Information of this type is generally available through Dunn and Bradstreet indices, professional trade associations, etc.

But these measurements aren't enough. The point of the analyses is *to determine how much profit you are making as a result of your C&C policies.* You must ask yourself some tough questions:

- What percentage of my sales are credit sales?

- What percentage of my sales would be lost if I eliminated credit?

- What percentage of my sales would be lost if I tightened credit?

- What percentage of my sales would be lost if I accepted only Grade-A credit risks?

- What percentage of my profits comes from credit sales?

- What percentage of my profits would be lost if I eliminated or tightened credit?

- What percentage of my profits would be lost if I accepted only Grade-A credit risks?

And perhaps the most important question of all:

- What measurement goals should I set to help maximize credit profitability?[†]

There are no easy answers to these questions. But taking the easy way out and ignoring them won't make them go away.

BOTTOM LINE: C&C policies must be accurately and exhaustively measured to determine their effect on profitability. Do you know whether your policies do more harm than good?

[†]Examples: ''Bad debt as a percentage of A/R should be _____. Any higher than that and we lose too much money. Any lower then that and we're turning away too many profitable customers.''
You're concerned with aggregate—rather than individual account—profitability.

ISSUE #4: COMMUNICATING THE C&C POLICY

There are two issues here: the simple communication task and the big picture.

1. *The simple communication task.* Certainly, you need an individual who is responsible for communicating the C&C policy to people in your company. This person should make sure that every individual who has contact with customers (sales reps, customer service staff, delivery people, and so on) has a copy of the company policy, has read it and understands it. When questions come up, employees should be trained to answer them.

    This step is easy. Designating a responsible party requires a little delegation. No deep meditation.

2. *The big picture.* The real gut issue here is not communicating the C&C policy; it is communicating *how we, as a company, feel about the C&C function.* The effectiveness of the C&C department is a reflection of how company leaders value C&C and those who handle it.

SUPPORT CHECKLIST

Complete the following checklist, then ask yourself, "Do I support my C&C people? Is it a visible or invisible means of support?"

Yes	No	
___	___	Salespeople have their own individual outside phone lines. C&C staffers have to share phones or go through the switchboard.
___	___	Everybody cares about sales, customer service, etc. We don't appear to value C&C. We've never passed around an office memo praising—or even *acknowledging*—our C&C department and its successes.
___	___	Changes in credit and collection policies are announced in the sales department rather than the C&C department.
___	___	Top managers act as Rah! Rah! cheerleaders for the sales department. C&C gets a raw inspirational deal.
___	___	Sales managers and others are allowed to second guess, and in some cases override, C&C department decisions.
___	___	The C&C staff has the smallest offices and the worst equipment.
___	___	Salespeople have latitude in determining what potential customers to pursue. C&C staffers don't have the same autonomy when it comes to pursuing debtors.
___	___	Top managers grant credit to associates, friends, and so on, without C&C department input, but expect the C&C department to handle the account should the client default.
___	___	The C&C department is always the last to know.

SUPPORT CHECKLIST (Continued)

Yes	No

___ ___ C&C staffers have a clique of their own and don't feel comfortable attending other departmental and company functions.

___ ___ Salespeople don't have to get approval of their sales, but C&C staffers must have collection actions approved by higher management.

___ ___ C&C personnel do not have access to training and seminars.

___ ___ Promotional opportunities are limited in the C&C department.

___ ___ Salespeople have incentive pay, bonuses, contests, etc., to reward their sales success. The C&C staff is not rewarded for collection success.

___ ___ C&C staffers make the same salary or less than peers in other departments, despite the additional stress of collection work.

___ ___ When the company has sales contests, there is no consideration for the additional C&C work and risk involved.

BOTTOM LINE: Only top management can communicate the importance of the C&C department's work. Their actions speak louder than words.

AN ADDED PERSPECTIVE

If you were surprised to find that you don't *really* support the C&C function, don't be. Many of your peers find themselves in the same boat.

This problem usually stems from subconscious fear or anxiety about this area. Read the following quotes. If you agree with any of them, you're harming—rather than arming—your C&C staff.

- *"Credit and collections isn't really an important function—not like sales! I'd rather concentrate on the positive ..."*

  "Sales" means moving product out. "Credit and collections" means moving money in. Cash flow, not product flow, should be your bottom line.

- *"I hate to collect money. It's embarrassing!"*

  Collecting money should be embarrassing—but to your tardy *customers,* not to you. They are the ones who broke their contracts. Don't take emotional responsibility for the irresponsibility of others.

- *"I want to collect every dollar I have coming to me."*

  Put aggregate profits before blind persistence. Collecting money costs money (not to mention time, effort, and angst). Don't spend $1000 chasing a $50 debt.

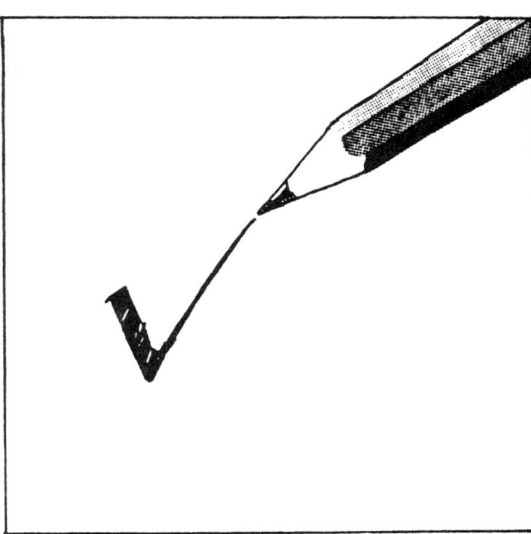

AN ADDED PERSPECTIVE (Continued)

- *"Sales and C&C mix about as well as oil and water."*

Actually, a strong C&C program facilitates sales. Let's look at both sides of the equation.

Credit: Many companies can't or won't pay cash for the items they buy. No credit, no sale.

Collection: If you don't collect on credit accounts, you can't afford to offer credit. If you don't offer credit...

- *"We hate collections because none of us likes to be mean to our customers."*

You don't have to be mean when collecting money. You just have to be firm—like you are in every other business function.

- *"We have to be very careful when we offer credit. We can't afford any bad debts."*

A better way to phrase this is, "We can't afford *too many* bad debts." If you only take customers with a 100 percent guarantee of payment, you'll miss out on the vast majority of customers and profits. The key to successful credit is determining at what risk-level profits are overtaken by expenses.

BOTTOM LINE: *C&C is not a drain on a business. It is a source of income and profit.* Treat it with courtesy and professionalism.

31

THE FINAL STEP

Look at your completed Form again. Use the information in this chapter to review and evaluate your current general administrative policies. Strategize, analyze, agonize, and compromise. Then, if appropriate, formalize by replacing your draft information with amended policies.

You're on the road to a more successful and profitable C&C system. Better bottom line or bust!

C H A P T E R

4

Cultural Concerns

NONASSERTIVE

ASSERTIVE

AGGRESSIVE

A C&C policy must recognize the corporate culture and integrate the culture's values into the policy. A laid-back work force isn't likely to be assertive with a customer when his account is 20 days past due. Employees who are used to strict controls won't be comfortable making ''instinct'' C&C decisions. A policy at odds with a culture isn't likely to get much organizational support.

This chapter is designed to help you explore your company's culture in four key areas, so that you can create a C&C policy that is custom-designed for your corporate environment.

ISSUE #1: PHILOSOPHICAL CREDIT RESTRICTIONS

Credit and collection strategies run the gamut from conservative (tight credit policy) to liberal (loose purse strings) to somewhere in between.

The following list will help you determine whether your C&C strategy should weigh in as conservative or liberal. Check all the conditions that are true of your company.

Check If This Is True	Condition	Optimal Strategy is Probably:	Rationale
☐	We want to open a lot of new accounts.	Liberal	There are only so many low-risk customers.
☐	We are in a very competitive industry.	Liberal	A loose credit policy may help take customers away from competitors.
☐	We are bringing out a lot of new products.	Liberal	Customers who are unsure of a product's salability—e.g., turnover and the resulting income—will need better credit terms.
☐	We have very high overhead.	Liberal	Lower your per-sale overhead costs by increasing the number of sales; increase the number of sales by loosening credit.
☐	We have a trendy product/service.	Liberal	Move the product while it's hot by offering good credit terms.
☐	Our product is past its prime.	Liberal	Move the product before it's too cold by offering good credit terms.
☐	We must have high sales volume.	Liberal	Credit facilitates sales, so loose credit leads to high volume.
☐	We have very high advertising costs.	Liberal	Advertising doesn't help if customers can't buy your product.
☐	We have high sales costs.	Liberal	The sales expense is for naught if customers can't buy your product.

Check If This Is True	Condition	Optimal Strategy is Probably:	Rationale
☐	We traditionally have high inventory levels.	Liberal	It's better to sell products on credit than have them sitting in the warehouse.
☐	We have a high profit margin.	Liberal	Our profit margin can absorb a relatively high level of losses.
☐	There is a greater demand for our product than there is supply.	Conservative	If you can pick and choose customers, choose to go with the less risky ones!
☐	We sell custom products.	Conservative	Custom products can't always be resold. You must be sure that the client will be around to pay for the product.
☐	Our product has a long production cycle.	Conservative	Couple a long production time with extended credit terms and you have excessive carrying charges.
☐	Our business is threatened by rough economic conditions (recession, depression, local layoffs, etc.).	Conservative	Customers are greater risks when there is more risk and uncertainty in the business environment.
☐	Our business is overextended.	Conservative	An overextended business can't afford to extend very much credit. Offering credit can be very expensive.
☐	We traditionally have low inventory levels.	Conservative	Reserve the product for low credit risks, because carrying charges, oversupply, etc., are not a problem.

BOTTOM LINE: Decisions on credit restrictions shouldn't be based—you might even say biased—on gut instinct. They should be based on objective business conditions.

ISSUE #2: ACTIVE OR PASSIVE C&C SYSTEM

Most C&C policies have at least a few promotional components, such as using fast-pay discounts to encourage fast payment. But you can do much more if your business culture is action-oriented.*

There are a number of actions that support good credit policies. For example, you should cultivate good relationships with your customers' accounts payable personnel. A/P clerks often decide which bills to pay and which to delay. A positive working relationship will prompt A/P people to pay your invoices first.

The following checklist will give you some ideas. Note the continuing emphasis on ''I'' and ''me.'' You're developing a personal relationship, not providing an impersonal service. For each practice, check whether you do this now, or whether you will now begin doing it.

I Do Now	I Will	
☐	☐	Get to know A/P people by name.
☐	☐	Develop a rapport with A/P people.
☐	☐	Ask A/P people what I can do to facilitate their job (for example, enclose documentation of delivery expenses, send additional invoice copies, etc.).
☐	☐	Let A/P people know that they can call me personally if they have a question or a problem, or if they need anything.
☐	☐	Thank A/P people personally when they help me resolve a payment problem.
☐	☐	Acknowledge a clerk's continuing excellence. (''I've noticed that you always have the check here on time.'')
☐	☐	Call and warn the A/P person when an unusually large bill is coming.
☐	☐	Acknowledge to the A/P person that he or she has a difficult job. Sympathize and empathize.
☐	☐	Let an A/P employee's manager know when he or she does a good job.
☐	☐	Never be rude to A/P people. They are just doing their job— and a hard one at that.

---

*Occasionally, you can find areas where a more passive approach would save C&C efforts without lessening C&C effectiveness. These, however, tend to be few and far between.

It pays to have a support system. It's doubly nice when that support system doesn't cost anything but a few nice words and courteous consideration.

BOTTOM LINE: When you review your C&C policy, look for areas where a more active approach would increase C&C efficiency. It makes sense to invest a little up-front effort when that effort will save time and money down the line.

ISSUE #3: DEBT-LEVEL DECISIONS AND YOUR AVERSION TO RISK

Debt levels are often set by the corporation's level of comfort, rather than by profitability goals. Fortunately this cultural component is elastic. People have debt discomfort when they're concerned about losing money. If you can demonstrate that a different debt level will add to profits, most of the ''cultural conflict'' will disappear.

However, that leaves another thorny problem. What debt level is the best debt level?

Don't set debt levels as a ratio or straight dollar figure. *That won't maximize profits.* The optimal debt level is at that point where *debt/sales expenses exceed debt/sales income.* In short, you should extend credit for as long as it is profitable to do so.

At every level of risk, there are customers who will pay and customers who won't. Let's say that, after careful analysis, you assign customers to a level of risk based on:

1. Your liberal/conservative risk comfort level

2. Their past payment record with your firm

3. Their credit history according to credit references, credit reporting services, etc.

4. Their unaudited financial statements

5. Their asset base

6. Your industry's credit history

DEFINING RISK GROUPS

You define the risk groups as follows:

- Level A customers are good as gold. 100 percent of them predictably pay 100 percent within 30 days.

- Level B customers are sterling silver. Historically, 80 percent of them pay 100 percent within 30 days; the other 20 percent pay within the next 30.

- Level C customers are somewhat tarnished. Your experience is that 75 percent of them pay 100 percent within 45 days, 20 percent pay most or all of their debt within the next 30 days, and 5 percent never pay the full invoice.

- Level D customers are the lead that drags down the accounts aging report. Only 70 percent pay most or all of the debt within 60 days, 20 percent pay most or all within the next 30, and 10 percent never make good the debt.

Once you have measurable risk categories, ask yourself:

- Where is the risk cutoff?
  - Do I offer credit to all customers in all four groups?
  - Do I offer credit to only a percentage of those customers in the C and D categories?
  - If so, what percentage?

- Where is the credit cutoff?
  - How much credit, on average, do I offer to individual businesses within each category?
  - How much outstanding debt will I carry in each category?

DEBT LEVEL DECISIONS (Continued)

The answer to these questions will depend on your individual business situation. Clearly, you offer credit to customers in levels A and B.* To determine the potential profit of level C and D customers, look at last year's sales figures.

- Determine the gross sales to level C customers. Don't forget to include both principal payments and interest/finance charges.

- Determine what expense amount can be attributed to level C sales. Include write-offs, write-downs, collection costs, financing costs (your cost of capital, etc.), as well as the ordinary business costs (product and delivery costs, overhead, etc.).

- If your level C income was higher than your level C costs, it makes sense to offer credit to level C customers. Ditto for D.

You can also plug in different numbers and generate sample scenarios. Based on past experience, what would your profits have been if you had offered level C customers 20 percent more credit? Or 20 percent less credit? Or offered credit to only 60% of the level C applicants?

> BOTTOM LINE: Temper your culture's strategic bias (liberal/conservative) with numerical analysis. You'll end up with a more profitable credit level.

---

*Assuming, of course, that your decision is based solely on risk and profitability factors and not on your own limited funds.

ISSUE #4: THE NEED FOR STRUCTURE

You've probably built part of your corporate culture around the success (or lack of success) you've had with structured systems.

Highly structured C&C systems certainly have advantages.

► They are easy to delegate. Employees simply follow the rules.

► They are inexpensive. Time-consuming decisions are waived in favor of the rulebook.

► They are easy to evaluate, because there are few variables to study.

► They are easy to explain: "No, sir, you aren't being singled out. We treat *everybody* this way!"

Of course, a highly structured system has its price.

► Customers expect to be treated as individuals. Treat them as categories and they'll take their business elsewhere.

► Strict guidelines lead to lower sales and fewer customers. Some profitable square pegs won't fit into your round holes.

► Highly structured systems often lead to morale and turnover problems. Many employees want to do their jobs as they think best.

► Highly structured systems are difficult to change. ("But we've always done it this way").

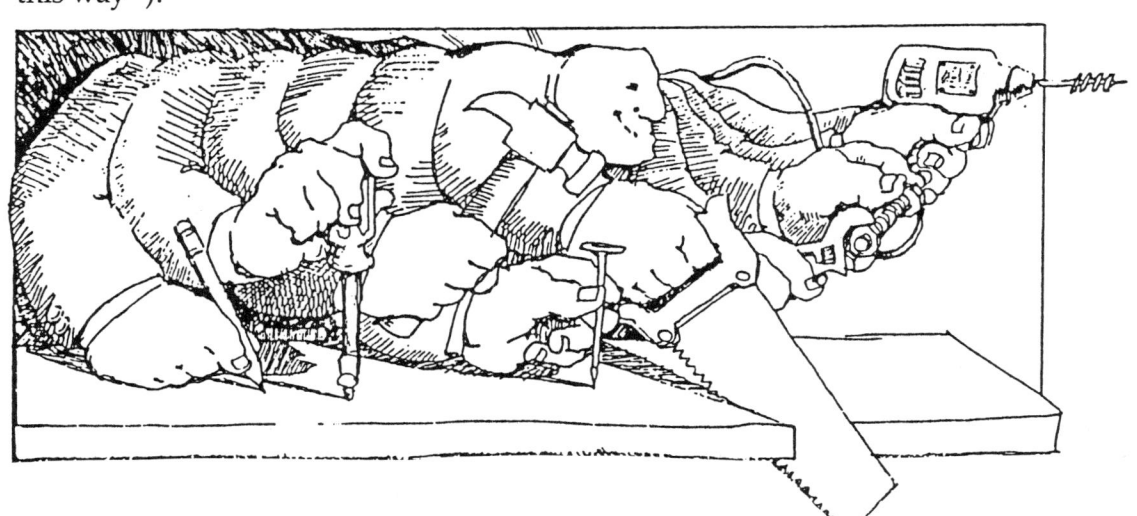

THE NEED FOR STRUCTURE (Continued)

You must determine the optimal level of system structure. Investigate every C&C function and procedure. Determine whether it needs more or less structure by asking:

- What are we trying to accomplish?

- Are we currently meeting this goal?

- Does our current approach/procedure help us meet this goal?

- Does our current approach/procedure work well? (For example, is it time- and cost-efficient?)

- Has our approach/procedure caused any problems?

- What do employees and managers think of our approach/procedure?

- Would they change it? If so, why or why not?

- What changes would they make?

Determine what level of structure you need and where you need it. Is your present structure being used constructively? Using structure for quality control is positive, but using structure for employee control is not.

BOTTOM LINE: C&C structure doesn't have to be an all-or-nothing kind of thing. A study of your C&C system will show you where structure makes sense...or nonsense.

THE FINAL STEP

Feeling cultured? Culture, like policy, reflects your state of mind.

Look again at your completed draft Form. Use the information in this chapter to review and evaluate your current policy. Strategize, analyze, agonize, and compromise. Then, if appropriate, formalize by replacing your draft information with amended policies in the "Cultural Concerns" section.

Combine your initial pearls of wisdom with the cultured pearls in this chapter and your system will be as sophisticated and rich as oysters Rockefeller!

"ANOTHER REVIEW OF 'THE FORM'
IS A GOOD IDEA"

C H A P T E R

5

The Credit Program

The issues in this chapter straddle both the planning and implementation sides of C&C policy. A successful billing and incentive system is the result of planning; you get increased cash flow when you implement a good billing/incentive system.

Dig into this chapter and see if you can unearth new ways to improve your C&C system. The harder you dig, the more likely you are to find pay dirt.

ISSUE #1: THE BILLING PROCESS

You probably already have your billing system down pat. If not, the rules are simple:

> Send complete and accurate invoices to clients ASAP and ask for complete, accurate, and immediate payment in return.

Unfortunately, many payment problems pop up at the invoice level. A lot of bills lack clarity. Most lack a sense of urgency. They promote confusion rather than payment.

Is your invoice a help or a hindrance? To evaluate the "payability" of your invoices, check yes or no for the criteria on the following checklist.

Yes	No	Criteria
☐	☐	We have an eye-catching invoice. It grabs visual attention.
☐	☐	We use the word "due" instead of "pay this amount."
☐	☐	We use big type on important words.
☐	☐	We enclose a preaddressed remittance envelope.
☐	☐	We enclose a stamped, preaddressed remittance envelope.
☐	☐	We list only one address on the bill.
☐	☐	Payments aren't accidentally sent to a warehouse or branch office address.
☐	☐	We don't list payment options on the bill.
☐	☐	We request full payment.
☐	☐	We send bills to a particular person.
☐	☐	We send A/P clerks all the invoice copies they need.
☐	☐	We send A/P clerks any documentation they need (for example, evidence of expenses, etc.)
☐	☐	We use colored envelopes to get customers' attention.

> BOTTOM LINE: Invoices are important because they generate most of your payments. Make them as strong and functional as possible to speed cash flow. Test your invoice by showing it to a non-business person. Can he or she figure out what it all means?

ISSUE #2: PAYMENT TERMS—DISCOUNTS, INTEREST, NET DUE

Payments terms have always packed a strong impact when it comes to influencing how and when customers pay. Unfortunately, many businesses set up payment terms without first setting up a strategy. If you want the most out of your payment terms while spending the least amount of money, you need to choose your terms wisely. Here are four specific recommendations.

1. Analyze your *specific* business environment. The payment plan you use must take into consideration:

- What others in your industry do

- What your customers want and ask for

- What you've done before

- What you want the payment plan to accomplish

- What tradeoff you're willing to make (such as money for time)

2. Analyze the *general* business environment. What payment terms would prompt early payment?

For example, let's say your payment terms are 2/10 net 60. You send XYZ, Ltd a bill for $1000. XYZ can pay $1000 in 60 days or $980 within 10 days. If they ignore the discount and pay the $1000 in 60 days, they have lost $20 and gained 50 days. Translation: XYZ paid $20 to use $980 for 50 days.

It cost XYZ, Ltd 2.04% to use the $980 ($20/$980). It only gained the use of that $980 for 50 days, or 50/365 of a year. Therefore, the 2.04% translates to an annual interest rate of 14.89% (2.04% divided by 50/365).

So what does this all mean? *If your customers can borrow money from a bank for less than 14.89%, they'll save money by borrowing from the bank to pay you.*

Always set discount rates at levels higher than the interest charged by banks. Ditto for interest charges on past due accounts. That way clients will pay your bills quickly because it makes economic sense to do so.

PAYMENT TERMS—DISCOUNTS, INTEREST, NET DUE (Continued)

3. Design safeguards into your payment incentive system.

- Make sure that discount rates are set high *but not too high.* If 14% annual interest would do the trick, don't get overgenerous and give customers 18%.

- Don't allow discounts on past-deadline payments. Inform the customer that your payment deadline was not met, so, in order to guarantee credit equality to all customers, the discount was disallowed.

- Stress that your discount program is not a *price discount* program. It is a *payment incentive* program.

- Determine when (or if) payment terms will be used as a negotiating tool. You may decide, for example, to waive interest charges if a long-term debtor agrees to pay his debt in full within 10 days.

4. Promote your program. Let customers know how much money they will save with immediate payments.

BOTTOM LINE: If an incentive program is going to work, you have to offer enough incentive. Design your payment terms with incentives in mind.

THE FINAL STEP

As we've seen, there's more to billing customers than merely sending out an invoice—that is, assuming you want them to pay their bills *now*.

Look once more at your completed Form. Use the information in this chapter to review and evaluate your current policies in the ''Credit Program'' section. Brainstorm improvements, then use them to amend your initial Form. If you want lightening-fast responses to your invoices, use techniques that merit thundering applause!

C H A P T E R

6

Acceptable Client Documentation

Common credit-granting procedures—asking clients to complete application forms, analyzing financial statements, contacting credit references, and obtaining credit reports—are nothing more than common sense, mere conventional wisdom.

Unfortunately, yesterday's conventional wisdom can create considerable trouble today. "Asking, analyzing, contacting, and obtaining" are not enough. You won't get the information you need to:

- Accurately assess an applicant's ability to meet the terms of his loan or account.

  or, *more importantly,*

- Detect frauds

A C&C department needs to think defensively.

BUT FIRST, A FEW WORDS ABOUT VERIFICATION

If you want to catch a rat, you have to play a game of cat and mouse. Actually, finding credit frauds (and simple information embellishers) isn't all that difficult. It just takes a little time—and a little patience.

The amount of time you spend researching a particular client, of course, will be affected by a number of factors: the age of the business (most frauds occur in "companies" less than three years old), size of account, and so on.

The cornerstone of verification is outside substantiation. You should try to corroborate every applicant's business and credit information through a second source—*one that can't be influenced/controlled by the applicant.* For example:

- The applicant lists his company's address and phone number on your application form. Do they jibe exactly with the information given in the phone book, zip code directory, etc.? Many frauds use legitimate business names to obtain credit. The goods, however, are diverted to an illegitimate address.

- The applicant says his company has been in business for six years. Does your state's Department of Commerce agree?

- When you compare the applicant's or business owner's Social Security number and/or EIN (Employer Identification Number) to government records, do the names and numbers match?

- Does the driver's license number the applicant gave *you* match the one your state Department of Motor Vehicles gave *him?*

In short, look for inconsistencies. If you find an applicant who fails to give you the truth, the whole truth, and nothing but the truth, you've probably found a fraud. No lie.

ISSUE #1: THE CREDIT APPLICATION

Most companies think of application forms as a mere formality. They're not. They serve two major functions:

1. To compile and document important information.

An example of *compiling:* In addition to standard credit information, application forms should require business owners or principals to list their Social Security numbers, driver's license numbers, residential phone numbers, emergency phone numbers, professional/trade license numbers (such as the P.E. number of a registered civil engineer), spouse's name/maiden name/Social Security number, etc. This makes it easier to locate "skips," those people who make a practice of skipping out without paying their debts.

An example of *documenting:* Application forms should list credit and payment terms, potential collection actions, etc. This gives your conditions and penalties more legal clout.

2. To detect fraud.

Application forms should request information and backup materials that applicants planning a fraud are not likely to have on hand.
Examples:

- Business cards

- Copies of professional certificates (Going back to our example of a civil engineer, can she provide a copy of her P.E. certificate?)

- Copies of legal documents (articles of incorporation, etc.)

- Copies of old tax returns prepared by a reputable CPA or attorney

- Marketing materials (Can our hapless civil engineer show us marketing brochures that feature her firm's past projects?)

Frauds seldom fake in-depth backup materials. There's too much work and money involved. Anybody with that level of patience and investment would probably go into a legitimate business!

BOTTOM LINE: A smart company uses its resources wisely. It recycles. In this case, it uses a resource—the credit application form—to fulfill two critical functions.

ISSUE #2: FINANCIAL REPORTS

Financial statements should provide the same two functions as application forms: to compile and document information, and to detect fraud.

1. To compile and document information.

Virtually every C&C department uses financial statements to take an applicant's financial temperature. This is done by figuring a firm's financial ratios and comparing them to relevant industry averages. For industry averages, see Dunn and Bradstreet industry indices at your local public library or your corporate library.

The basic financial ratios to calculate and compare are:

Current ratio	which is	$\dfrac{\text{assets (current)}}{\text{liabilities (current)}}$
Quick ratio	which is	$\dfrac{\text{cash + marketable securities + A/R}}{\text{liabilities (current)}}$
Debt ratio	which is	$\dfrac{\text{total liabilities}}{\text{total assets}}$
Receivables turnover	which is	$\dfrac{\text{sales (net)}}{\text{average receivables}}$
Inventory turnover	which is	$\dfrac{\text{Sales cost}}{\text{inventory}}$

If analyzing and comparing the ratios on the facing page is all your C&C department does, it isn't doing enough. You need to dig beneath the surface. Do the figures used in these ratios reflect reality?

For example, does the company classify returns as inventory? Returns may be used, broken, out of style, no longer in demand, etc. Is this taken into account in the inventory turnover valuation?

Remember, garbage in, garbage out. Don't accept a ratio unless you can reliably accept the variables that went into it.

2. To detect fraud.

If you require a current *audited* financial statement, you will deter many frauds. For additional protection, insist that the applicant submit monthly financial statements that are:

- Signed by all business owners/principals

- Witnessed by a second party

- Notarized by a notary public

- Sent by registered mail through the U.S. Post Office

Why the heavy-handedness? Frauds don't want their illegal behavior on record. This level of legal documentation will scare away even the most confident con person.

> BOTTOM LINE: Financial statements tell about more than just finances. If you pay attention, they can also warn you about potential frauds.

ISSUE #3: CREDIT REFERENCES

Again, you need to make sure that a business formality—obtaining credit references—is used to compile and document important information and spot frauds. However, this time the effort really gets interesting.

Let's take this one step at a time. First, acknowledge reality. Applicants pick and choose their credit references. It's not likely they'll pass on a negative one. Therefore, don't use an applicant's credit references *as credit references*. Instead, use them to:

- Find other, older credit references

- Identify potential fraud

Let's see how this applies to our two primary functions.

1. To compile and document important information.

Replace the applicant's hand-picked credit references with more legitimate informers. You should:

- Ask the applicant where he buys items that are not sold by his credit references. (''I notice you don't have an office supply firm down as a credit reference. Where you do you buy your office supplies?'') Contact these stores and ask questions such as these:

  - Does my applicant have a credit account? Why/why not?

  - What is my applicant's current credit line? Why isn't it higher?

  - How high is my applicant's current account balance?

  - What is my applicant's average monthly balance?

  - How long has my applicant held this account?

- Call the credit references that the applicant has listed. Ask them for the company names your applicant gave them as credit references. Call those earlier companies and see if your applicant still rates a good word.

If these two techniques generate positive credit references, you've probably got yourself a winner.

2. To detect fraud.

Review the credit references you were given. Look for signs of a swindle. For example:

- Credit references that are only listed by phone number, address, or post office box

- Reference companies you've never heard of

- Reference companies that aren't listed in the phone book

- Reference that the applicant delivers with his application form

- Business references that don't sound businesslike (the "receptionist" answers the phone by saying "Hello"; you can hear small children, animals, or kitchen appliances in the background; there is only one employee on the premises, etc.)

BOTTOM LINE: Be pushy when it comes to finding hidden credit references. Don't be a pushover for applicant-supplied sources.

CHECK YOUR REFERENCES

ISSUE #4: CREDIT REPORTING COMPANIES

Credit reports from reputable credit reporting companies are a tremendous C&C tool. They aren't indispensable. They aren't 100 percent reliable. But they are another excellent means to improve your C&C practices—that is, if you use them wisely.

Here are recommendations for using credit reports to achieve your two goals:

1. To compile and document information.

A credit reporting company's primary function is to gather and repeat information. It couldn't possibly empirically verify all the data it receives annually. So don't use credit reports to make critical financial decisions. Use them to double-check information on applications, financial statements, credit references, etc.

2. To detect fraud.

You can also use credit reports to spot potential frauds. For example:

- Pay special attention to any unusual credit information (many requests for the applicant's credit report, a lot of credit secured in a short time, far more new accounts than one would expect, etc.).

- Look for inconsistencies and oddities (for example, the credit report lists a different address for the applicant than you have on file).

> BOTTOM LINE: Credit reports are an excellent resource but not a stand-alone information source. Use them judiciously.

THE FINAL STEP

Remember—of course you remember!—the two goals we've been following since the beginning of this chapter? The goals for all credit documentation are:

1. To compile and document information.

2. To detect fraud.

When you review the ''Acceptable Client Documentation'' section of your Form, don't forget these two goals and the recommendations discussed in this chapter. Make sure that your amended Form takes both goals into account. That's creative accounting.

C H A P T E R

7

Risk Control

It's not enough to protect yourself from frauds. You also need to protect yourself against other firms' fiascoes, foibles, and failures.

There are two kinds of risk control worth pursuing. You can get:

- Additional safeguards from *inside* the buyer/supplier relationship through such things as personal guarantees

- Safeguards from *outside* the buyer/supplier relationship in the form of credit insurance, irrevocable letters of credit from a bank, etc.

Either, or both, of these controls should be a part of your C&C practices.

ISSUE #1: INSIDE SAFEGUARDS

When you ask a buyer to provide inside safeguards (personal guarantees, cosigners for loans, etc.), you're not asking for trouble. You're asking because you want to *avoid* trouble.

Still, this is a tricky issue. Buyers may refuse to cooperate. (''I trust you enough to buy your product; however, you don't trust me enough to offer unsecured credit.'') Then what do you do?

There are two difficulties inherent in obtaining inside safeguards. Both have to be handled diplomatically.

1. *Asking for the safeguard.* When you ask for an inside safeguard, don't make the request sound oppressive or personal in nature. Explain that it's simply a routine procedure: ''I need a personal guarantee from you because ...''

- Your company is less than five years old

- Your such-and-such financial ratio is lower than industry average

- Your business is a single proprietorship

- Your credit history runs less than two years

Add, ''I am required to get personal guarantees from *all* applicants who share this particular characteristic.''

Don't single applicants out for special scrutiny. Treat comparable customers equitably. They can't legitimately fight against fairness.

2. *Ensuring the value of the safeguard.* Having a safeguard is worthless if the safeguard you have is worthless. You can get a personal guarantee from a business owner, but it's not worth squat if fifty other businesspeople got one first. A collateral pledge isn't worth the paper it's written on if the credit applicant has virtually no equity in the asset. A cosigned loan is meaningless if the cosigner is in worse shape than the applicant.

In short, verify inside safeguards with the same tenacity you use to verify other credit-granting information.

> BOTTOM LINE: Inside safeguards—*well-drafted* inside safeguards—are worth considering because they can give you the inside track on debt protection.

VERIFY YOUR SAFEGUARDS

ISSUE #2: OUTSIDE SAFEGUARDS

Are you a betting person? Here's the game.

Outside safeguards—credit insurance, irrevocable letters of credit, etc.—cost you. Guaranteed. Credit insurance will cost you a percentage of your credit sales.* Customers who provide you with an irrevocable letter of credit will insist on lower product prices, better payment terms, etc., to defray the LC's cost.

Outside safeguards can save you, save you *big*. An irrevocable LC covers potential losses from an individual customer. Credit insurance can cover a great deal more: substantial losses due to the bankruptcy of a major credit client, a regional recession, niche industry depression, etc.

Are you willing to pay a little and maybe save a lot? Or do you want to save every dime you can, even if it eventually costs you big bucks? Only you can decide.

Make an informed decision. For credit insurance decision data:

- Contact credit insurance salespeople and access their risk data.

- Find out if credit insurance is standard practice in your industry.

- Calculate your costs and payback if you had been a credit insurance customer over the last five years.

For data on irrevocable LCs:

- Talk to local banks. What will an irrevocable LC cost your clients?

- Can you help customers make a cut-rate irrevocable LC deal through your own bank?

> BOTTOM LINE: Research outside safeguards. An ounce of prevention is usually worth the effort and expenses.

---

*The premium percentage will vary depending your business' (and your industry's) past collection record, customer risk record, current economic trends, etc.

† Coverage amounts and exemptions, of course, are different for each policy. If you decide to buy credit insurance, make sure it covers what you want and need.

THE FINAL STEP

You probably haven't spent a great deal of time thinking or planning about inside or outside safeguards. You probably haven't spent much money on them, either.

When you refer back to the ''Risk Control'' section of your Form, ask yourself one question: ''Do I want to put my faith in my customers or in additional safety measures?'' Keep your answer in mind when you amend the Form. You may find that inside and outside safeguards have a profitable side.

C H A P T E R

8

Collection Systems

In a triumph of hope over experience, most of us dream of finding that magic collection technique that will make all past-due accounts collectible. This chapter should probably be subtitled "The Chapter Most Likely to Be Read."

That's unfortunate, because paying more attention to the credit half of the C&C equation greatly reduces a business's need for costly and stressful collection actions.

Still, even companies with superlative credit systems eventually face a collections problem. There are basically six phases in the collection of late payments.

ISSUE #1: PROBLEM IDENTIFICATION SYSTEM

Most small businesses use an accounts aging (AA) report to identify seriously past-due balances. Unfortunately, most AA reports merely list past-due accounts; they don't provide enough assistance for collection. The acid test: Does your AA report graphically point out problems, or do you have to find them yourself? For example:

1. Are problem accounts highlighted in a different color?

2. Are accounts listed by problematic components such as:

- Age

- Total amount past due

- Percentage of account 120 days or more past due (The critical day count could be 90 or 60, depending on your cash flow needs.)

You should generate multiple AA reports, each focusing on a different critical criteria. Accounts should be listed in descending order with the critical category's worst offender at the top.

3. Do you generate an AA for each C&C staffer, listing only his or her accounts? This helps identify both problem accounts and problem staff people.

4. Is there a comment column for listing collection activities and dates? This assists in following up and analyzing individual accounts, and also provides data on the overall system. (Are collection actions being taken at predetermined times?)

BOTTOM LINE: Your AA report should tell you what you need to know at a glance. You shouldn't have to dig for vital information.

ISSUE #2: COLLECTION ACTIONS—
THE FIRST STEP

Hard truth: There is no 100%-effective C&C form letter. There is no 100%-effective collection call format. If there were, they would develop a cult following. Everybody would use them and they would quickly lose their punch.

There are guidelines for writing effective collection letters and making effective collection calls. *However, knowing these guidelines is only half the battle. You have to know when to use them.*

Determine which collection action generates the most cash flow. Is it:

• The first collection action, regardless of what it is?

• A second copy of the original invoice?

• The first collection letter?

• The second collection letter?

• The first collection call?

• The second collection call?

• The first time you mention legal action, regardless of the contact format?

Look back through your C&C records. If the collection action that generates the most money is the first collection call, *take that action sooner in the collection cycle.*

Second copies of the original invoice may cost less than a phone call. Collection letters may be less expensive, too. But if they don't collect large sums of money, they're a false economy. You want to do what works, not what's cheap.

> BOTTOM LINE: Don't settle for a particular collection system just because it's easy or cheap. C&C profits—not C&C costs—are the best measurement of a successful system.

ISSUE #3: COLLECTION LETTERS

While there's no perfect collection letter, there are some perfectly good guidelines for effectiveness. If a collection letter fills the following criteria, it's fulfilling your objectives. Your letter should be:

- Above all, *readable.* If it isn't readable, clients won't read it. If they don't read it, it can't do its job. Readable letters meet the other criteria on this list.

- *Clear.* Could the reader paraphrase your letter to a second party?

- *Concise.* One page is always long enough.

- *Interesting.* Does it tell the reader something he really wants to know or should think about?

- *Personal.* Do you read the form letters other people send you?

- *Accurate.* Does the client really owe what you say he owes?

- *Easy on the eyes.* Short words and paragraphs, lots of white space, etc.

- *Firm and authoritative.* Note that firm is not synonymous with threatening.

- *Reasonable.* For example, does it explain why you are about to turn this matter over to your lawyer?

- *Instructive.* Ask the client to send you some money *today.*

- *Final.* It should tell the client in an objective manner exactly what will happen and/or what you will do if your request for payment is not met.

For a sample collection letter, see page 76.

> BOTTOM LINE: If a collection letter is all of the above, it's probably also effective.

ISSUE #4: COLLECTION CALLS

Phone calls are probably your most effective collection action. They generate immediate feedback. They allow for a meaningful dialogue. You know when and if you've reached the party in question.

For successful collection calls:

1. *Listen to the customer.*

2. Make sure you cover all of the pertinent information. Before you make your call, gather all the necessary information. For example:

- Vendor name/address/phone (for verfication)
- Total amount due
- Amount past due
- When the debt was due
- Previous collection actions taken
- Previous promises made/broken by the debtor
- Actions that will be taken unless...

To circumvent stalling, you should also have order information on hand:

- Purchase order number/purchaser name
- Item(s) purchased
- Item prices
- Extra charges (shipping, overnight express, insurance as per customer request, etc.)
- Item shipment date
- Item delivery date

3. Follow up. No matter what the client promises, keep track of his or her actions. A promise isn't the same as a payment.

4. Don't leave messages. Leaving messages with the wrong people, implying that an individual owes you money, can generate lawsuits.

NOTE: For a sample phone call, see page 77.

BOTTOM LINE: Prep work is what makes collection calls work.

ISSUE #5: DEVIANT DEBTOR BEHAVIOR

Some customers consistently come up with payments; others consistently come up with excuses.

There are an infinite number of excuses: the product doesn't do what you said it would, I didn't get what I ordered, the shipment took too long, we are planning to return the product, I didn't get an invoice, etc. Fortunately, this infinite number of excuses can be handled by one fine—and finite—process. Here are the basics.

- Determine whether the excuse is legitimate. Can the problem be documented? Was the complaint raised before or after you contacted the client? Is the excuse (or client) believable?

- Determine whether the excuse is sufficient reason to withhold payment. Some problems may justify withholding payment. Many don't. "I didn't pay because your staff was rude to me" doesn't change the fact that the debtor received a product and must pay for it.

- Measure the problem. Let's say a customer refuses to pay because a shipment was damaged in transit. Exactly what does "damaged" mean? All of the goods were damaged? Half of the goods were damaged?

  The box was dinged? If only 5 percent of the shipment was damaged and needs to be returned shouldn't the customer use—and pay for—the other 95 percent?

- Figure out what it would take to resolve the problem. How does the client think this matter should be resolved? Can you negotiate a compromise between the two perspectives?

- Resolve the problem. *Now.* Don't let C&C problems drag on and on. The Commercial Law League of America found that $1 past due is only worth 94¢ after a month; that value drops to 74¢ after two months and 58¢ after six months. Waiting is not in your best interest.

  Do what it takes to remedy the situation. Waive interest charges if that will prompt a payment. Set up an installment pay plan. Take 80¢ on the dollar if you have to. *But resolve the problem.* There's no time like the present if you want to save any semblance of profit.

BOTTOM LINE: Client excuses are no excuse for letting past due accounts accumulate. Don't head the other way when you hear an excuse. Meet it head on.

ISSUE #6:
THE LAST-DITCH DEPARTMENT

It happens to the best—as well as the worst—of us. We eventually run into customers who have no intention of paying their bills. Absolutely none.

So how do you handle this kind of situation? The answer is: you don't. In such a case, you consider three options:

- Turning the account over to a collection agency

- Turning the account over to an attorney who specializes in collection work

- Writing off the account

Turn the account over to a collection agency if:

- You think they can collect. The threat of having a collection agency referral on their credit records prompts some purchasers to pay.

- The required collection effort justifies the hefty collection fee.

- You don't want to sink any more out-of-pocket money into the account. Collection agencies usually work on a contingency fee basis.

- The unpaid balance is worth the effort.

THE LAST-DITCH DEPARTMENT (Continued)

Turn the account over to an attorney if:

- The debtor will be intimidated enough by a "lawyer letter" to pay quickly.

- The lawyer can collect your money via a letter or a call or two. Remember, your lawyer is going to charge you by the hour!

- The account balance justifies investing additional collection expenses.

- You may eventually take the case to court.

Write the account off if:

- The costs of collecting outweigh the potential gain.

BOTTOM LINE: When you're dealing with uncollectible accounts, make business—rather than emotional—decisions. It's better to throw a bad account away than to throw good money after bad.

THE FINAL STEP

If you want a successful collection system, you must focus on two issues:

• When will specific actions be taken?

• How can a specific action be made as effective as possible?

Refer to your original Form. Are these two issues addressed in the "Collection Systems" section of your written guidelines? If not, make sure they are a part of your amended Form—that is, if you are amenable to additional profits and decide to mend your ways.

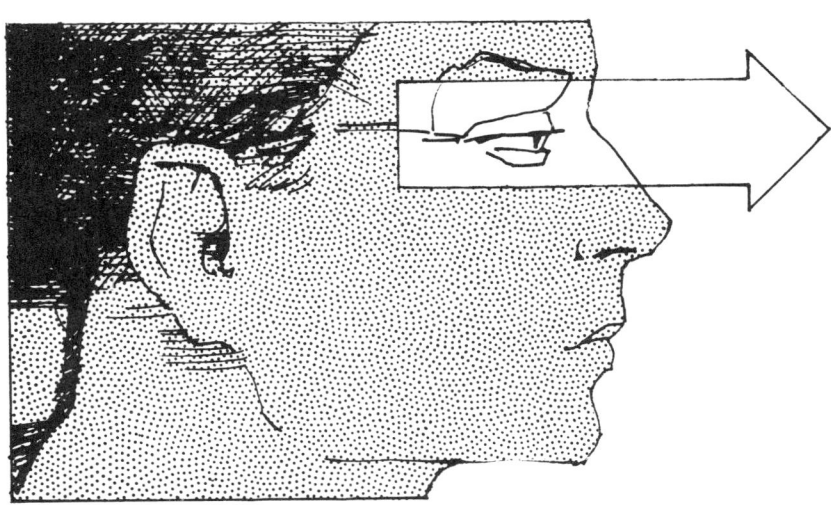

SAMPLE COLLECTION LETTER

John Smith
Smith's
100 Main St.
Anywhere, U.S.

Dear Mr. Smith:

You've owed us $1000 since 6/1—but I'm not writing to rehash something you already know. I'm writing to tell you something you may not know. I owe it to you.

If we do not receive your $1000 payment by 8/15 this matter will be turned over to the ABC Collection Agency. You should ask your credit and collections manager how such an action would affect your credit rating and business operations.

A collection agency action taints your entire business. Cautious vendors will require money up front or charge higher prices to offset the risk of doing business with you. Banks will be less willing to loan you operating capital. A bad credit history can make it difficult to obtain long-term equipment, maintenance, or office leases.

You have two debts to pay. You owe us $1000 and you owe yourself a good credit record. Pay us by 8/15 and you'll cancel two debts for the price of one.

Professionally,

Mary Doe
Accounts Receivables Manager

Enc. (debt documentation)

SAMPLE COLLECTION CALL

Debtor: Hello?

You: Hello. Is this John Smith of Smith's, 100 Main St., Anywhere U.S.?

Debtor: Yes. Who's this?

You: I'm Mary Smith, Accounts Receivables Manager at Acme Widgets. I'm calling about invoice #12345 dated May 1. There's an outstanding balance on your account of $1030.

Debtor: I don't remember buying anything from you.

You: According to my records, you ordered 10 mega-monster widgets from us on May 1 using purchase order number #555. The unit price on each mega-monster was $90. There was an additional shipping charge of $10 per unit. Finance charges of $30 have brought the total amount due to $1030.

The units were shipped on May 1 and, according to my copy of the delivery roster, arrived on May 3. Someone with the initials "JS" signed for them.

Debtor: Oh, I remember now. I don't think I ever got an invoice for those.

You: The first invoice was mailed on May 1. A second invoice was mailed on June 1. We sent a personal letter and third invoice on June 15. If you give me your fax number, I'll fax another invoice so that you can process payment today.

Debtor: Well, I don't have a fax machine. Even if I did, I wouldn't pay the $1000.

You: Why not?

*"IT ALL STARTS WITH
THE TONE OF YOUR VOICE"*

SAMPLE COLLECTION CALL (Continued)

Debtor: I don't have that kind of extra cash in the company checking account. I've got to meet payroll, pay my taxes, pay the rent...

You: How much do you have?

Debtor: Well, I could probably send you a check for $100.

You: It sounds like we need to set up an installment plan. How does this sound: You send me a check today for $100. Then, for the next nine months, you send me a monthly check for $105 to cover payments on the principal and related finance charges. I'll expect your check no later than the fifth of each month.

This way, you can work on your account balance, I can avoid sending this invoice to a collection agency.

Debtor: I think I can do that.

You: If you think this plan could cause problems, please tell me now. I need you to sign a contract formalizing our agreement. It will become part of your permanent collection file. If you fail to make the payments as agreed, the matter will immediately be sent to a collection agency.

Debtor: Yes, I can do it.

You: Great. I'll mail you two copies of the payment plan. Keep a copy for your files and send a signed copy back to me. Then we're in business!

Debtor: Goodbye.

You: Goodbye.

BOOK SUMMARY

Before you read this book, you had a C&C policy. It may have been a policy of "no credit." Or "no credit until we know you better." Or "notoriously free credit." Wherever it stood, it was a good place to start.

That starting place has led to an even better C&C system. The Credit and Collection Policies Compilation Form on page 11 helped you put your current policy in writing. As you finished each chapter of this book, you reviewed your Form subject by subject, issue by issue.

When appropriate, you amended your written policy to improve its efficiency and effectiveness. To review the key points:

- *General administrative issues.* Make sure your system is something that grows and changes with your business, the economy, customer needs, and so on. Design a strategy, not a straitjacket.

- *Cultural concerns.* A system works best when it works within a business's cultural confines. Work with, rather than against, your people, practices, and perspectives.

- *Credit program.* Develop a system that encourages—rather than discourages—prompt payments. Emphasize the positive (good payment terms) rather than the negative (tough collection policies).

- *Acceptable client documentation.* The credit approval process (credit applications, credit references, etc.) should be the focal point of any C&C program. The time to identify high-risk customers and frauds is before you offer them credit, not after.

- *Risk control.* An ounce of protection is worth a pound of cure. Consider extra measures to ensure the collectibility of accounts. It's usually worth the effort and the investment.

- *Collection systems.* The best collection system is a good credit system. Still, bad accounts—like the common cold—occasionally invade the system. Make sure that your C&C department follows up on foul-ups in a timely and effective way.

Your amended "Credit and Collection Policies Compilation Form" is more than a mental exercise. It is a basic component of fiscal fitness: a written C&C policy.

There you have it, what you need for a good running start at a top C&C system. Now all you have to do is take the ball and run with it!

NOTES

FOR OTHER FIFTY-MINUTE SELF-STUDY BOOKS
SEE THE BACK OF THIS BOOK.

$$\boxed{\text{NOTES}}$$

FOR OTHER FIFTY-MINUTE SELF-STUDY BOOKS
SEE THE BACK OF THIS BOOK.

NOTES

FOR OTHER FIFTY-MINUTE SELF-STUDY BOOKS
SEE THE BACK OF THIS BOOK.

NOTES

FOR OTHER FIFTY-MINUTE SELF-STUDY BOOKS
SEE THE BACK OF THIS BOOK.

NOTES

FOR OTHER FIFTY-MINUTE SELF-STUDY BOOKS
SEE THE BACK OF THIS BOOK.

NOTES

FOR OTHER FIFTY-MINUTE SELF-STUDY BOOKS
SEE THE BACK OF THIS BOOK.

NOTES

FOR OTHER FIFTY-MINUTE SELF-STUDY BOOKS
SEE THE BACK OF THIS BOOK.

We hope you enjoyed this book. If so, we have good news for you. This title is part of the best-selling *FIFTY-MINUTE*™ *Series* of books. All *Series* books are similar in size and identical in price. Several are supported with training videos (identified by the symbol ⓥ next to the title).

FIFTY-MINUTE Books and Videos are available from your distributor. A free catalog is available upon request from Crisp Publications, Inc., 1200 Hamilton Court, Menlo Park, California 94025.

FIFTY-MINUTE Series Books & Videos organized by general subject area.

Management Training (continued):

Personal Improvement:

Human Resources & Wellness:

Human Resources & Wellness (continued):

Communications & Creativity:

Customer Service/Sales Training:

Small Business & Financial Planning:

Adult Literacy & Learning:

Career/Retirement & Life Planning: